Made me laugh, cry and remember my first love, childhood, coming out again and again, closets and keys, secrets and stepping stones.
- Catrina McHugh, Joint CEO, Artistic Director and Writer of Open Clasp Theatre Company

Despite their differences, the characters share similar feelings and anxieties about coming out - first to themselves and then again (and again and again) to those around them. Essential reading for all teens, it deserves a place in every school library.
- Sophie Masztalerz, School Librarian

There was something new and special on every page of this book that made me not want to stop reading.
- Ryan Vale, Author of Holy Water

Not/Coming Out
A Charity Anthology

Not/Coming Out
A Charity Anthology

Contributing Authors

Nil Digante - Colin Brooks - Katherine Shaw
Priscilla Kint - Breanna Guinta - Airic Fenn
Samantha Maich - Robyn Hill - Emily Byars
Sarah Fletchins - Sky DuVall – A. Lynn Rosefinch
Hannah Rose - Brandon Shane - Daniel Skentelbery
Kate Foot - Florence-Susanne Reppert - Felix Graves

Content warnings: this anthology contains references to homophobia,
transphobia, coming out, and mental health. Some individual pieces are
introduced with their additional content warnings.

This is the Standard Edition

ISBN: 978-1-914210-99-0
Thank you, Macfarlane Lantern Publishing, for supporting this anthology.

Foreword

It's true that coming out doesn't just happen once: it is a constant process that is different for everyone. We want this anthology to show that, wherever in this process you are, you are welcome.

The idea for this anthology was born out of a Twitter prompt challenge. Now, looking at this finished book, we're reminded how talented and powerful LGBTQ+ writers are.

Copies of this anthology will be sent to schools and community groups, especially those which support LGBTQ+ youth. We hope to inspire young writers to tell their stories without fear.

Royalties from the sale of Not/Coming Out will be donated to akt, a UK charity that supports LGBTQ+ young people at risk of experiencing homelessness.

The mainstream media may be indulging in culture wars, but there is hope out there. Hope that you are not alone. Hope that you have a community, whether you are openly part of it or not. Hope that your story is worth telling.

-    Amanda, Dewi, Kenzie and Lou

Contents

We Exist
Nil Digante

CW: drowning, erasure

We exist

In the small crevices where dandelions grow
In the rushing of a river to a sea
In the silent void of space where no one will ever know

We exist

In the dimple of a lover, soft and sweet
In the swirling of soft white clouds high above
In the pages of a book, edges crisp and sharp and neat

We exist

In the backyards memories of childhood homes
In the bright, loud parades down in the city
In the buried dirt covering our ancestors' forgotten bones

We exist

Not/Coming Out

In the water that drowns us in graves so cold
In the voices that history erased
In the fire that burns in our blood, our bones, our heart,
our soul

We exist

Polka Dots and Moonbeams
Colin Brooks

CW: alcohol

It was a mystery why I'd shown up to the dance at all.

As I stood atop the concrete steps, surveying the crowd below maneuvering through North Virginia College's garden courtyard, I realized it was the last place I wanted to be. I could make out some of my classmates in the dim outdoor light – a mix of soft yellow lantern light and bright moonlight from above – dancing with their dates to the music coming from the band in the corner, a jazz tune I didn't know. A banner hung from two marble pillars nearby that said, "Bon Voyage, Class of 1946!". The guys wore a lot of the same things: pinstriped suits in various dark blues and blacks with white shirts and patterned ties, while their dates' dresses varied in patterns and bright colors.

Being dateless had been one of the main reasons why I'd wanted to skip, but my buddies in the dormitory had begged me to go anyway. I'd never tell them this, but it wasn't that I was upset I didn't have a girl to go with; it was that I didn't want one. I'd tried going with girls before, trying desperately to feel something, anything, but it never clicked for me like it did when I was around classmates on campus at the men's college. My roommate, Eugene, liked to rag on me in front of the guys about it, but he thought it was because I was shy. It wasn't true, but I let him think it anyway. It was easier for everyone that way.

'Roy, buddy!'

I turned, eyeing the gang coming towards me – Eugene, Norman, Stanley, and Jimmy – leaning on each other as they walked and looking obviously sauced. Like the others, they were dressed in dark pinstriped suits, all wearing ties except for Stanley, who bore a blue-gray bowtie that matched his jacket. Despite my dark mood, I cracked a grin as they moved my way. I knew them well, all roommates and neighbors in our dormitory hall. When they were close enough, I knew exactly what Jimmy'd say before he could even open his mouth.

'What's buzzin', cousin?' he asked, slightly slurring.

'You know you've said the same thing to me every time we've seen each other for the last four years?' I said, laughing when he ran an embarrassed hand through his thick blond hair.

'Yeah, what do you know…' he grumbled.

'You been here long, Roy?' Eugene asked, elbowing Jimmy out of the way. I shrugged. 'Not long. Didn't feel like dancing much yet.'

'Eyed any good-looking broads around here?' Norman asked, looking at the crowd over my shoulder. He was a handsome guy with dark features and could easily find an available girl to go with, but always liked to go for those already with a date. He claimed each time was an honest mistake, but after the fourth time, I figured he must like the trouble it caused.

'Some,' I lied, looking away toward a bush to my left. 'Haven't been here very long.'

'Let's go check it out, then,' Norman replied, clapping a heavy hand on my arm. He led the way down the steps, the rest of us falling in line behind him, splitting up once we were on the floor.

Norm immediately cut in on a couple's dance, swaying to the music with a dark-haired girl in a plum-colored dress while her date scowled at them from a few feet away. Eugene and Jimmy, bumping into each other as they walked, approached a group of three women – two blondes that looked to be related and a redhead, who were deep in a conversation of their own.

'You going to find someone to dance with?' Stanley asked, turning to me.

'Don't feel like it right now,' I replied, shrugging again. 'Think I'm gonna go smoke instead.'

'Mind if I join you?'

I nodded, walking across the garden to a spot I liked to sit by myself. I'd discovered it my second year at NVC and hadn't told anyone; a secluded area against the side of one of the brick buildings the garden sat next to, surrounded by tall bushes with a small stone bench against the brick, as if made for a secret rendezvous. At first glance, it just looked like a random assortment of foliage, but it made for a great spot to smoke or study in peace if you knew how to get to it.

Twigs cracked under our shoes as we made our way over to the thicket, stopping just before the hidden entrance. I looked around, making sure the coast was clear, and pushed a low-hanging branch out of the way, revealing the hideaway. Stanley let out a low, impressed whistle, ducking under the branch and looking around. It wasn't much, just some open space and the gray stone bench, but he seemed fascinated just the same.

'I never knew this was here,' he said, keeping his voice low.

'Don't think many people do,' I replied, matching his quiet tone.

I sat, feeling the cold stone meet the seat of my pants, and pulled the small red cigarette box from my pocket. We could still hear the band from where we were, though the music was faint, and Stanley swayed this way and that to the soft beat of the drums as he moved to sit next to me on the bench. It wasn't very large, so Stanley and I were suddenly very close as he sat down, our knees touching.

I felt my heart beat faster and ignored it, fiddling with the lid of the cigarette container. Finally getting it open, I pulled one out and placed it between my lips, turning to Stanley and pointing the box toward him. Carefully, he reached in and grabbed one, his thumb brushing mine while he did. Again, I ignored my accelerating heartbeat, refusing to look at Stanley as I pulled out a match.

Sitting this close, I could smell the liquor on his breath, but I didn't mind it. He smelled of lavender and some sort of spice, earthy and warm and inviting. I took a deep breath, hoping to calm my pounding heart, and my nose was filled with Stan.

I turned slightly toward him so there was a small bit of stone available and struck the match against it, earning a small flame on the end of it. I quickly raised it to my cigarette, inhaling until the flame caught on the end. While I was watching to make sure the cigarette burned, the flame lowered on the match until it was just above my fingers. I hissed, the heat biting at my fingertips, and shook the match until the flame was extinguished, crushing it underneath my shoe to be sure.

'That was my last one. You don't happen to have a match, do you?' I asked, glancing quickly at Stan.

Out of all the guys in our group, I found Stanley to be the most attractive, so it was torture to be this close. He was handsome, with thick-framed glasses and dark brown hair, but smart and funny without being obnoxious about it like Eugene was.

Stanley chuckled, smile lines appearing on each cheek. 'No, I don't. Here, let me.'

He leaned in, our faces inches from one another, and placed the end of his cigarette against the end of mine until embers began to burn red at the end of his too, all

7

the while looking at me. He pulled away, keeping eye contact, and let out a puff of smoke.

My throat clicked as I swallowed, suddenly very dry.

'So what's your beef with dancing, Roy?' he asked after a moment of tense silence.

My eyebrows raised in surprise. 'I don't have any beef with dancing. I just didn't want to, that's all.'

'That's what you said at the last dance, too. You sure?' he asked, a smirk playing on his lips.

'What about you? You're not dancing either.'

He sighed, placing his hands above his head and looking towards the star-filled sky. 'Yeah, well, I'm not in the mood to deal with any dames tonight. You know what I mean?'

'I guess so,' I said noncommittally, following his lead and looking towards the sky. I took a puff and blew the smoke upward, watching as it disappeared amid the stars.

'I think you do, Roy.'

I turned to look at him, making sure to do so slowly, hopefully somewhat naturally, so as not to give anything away. He was already looking at me, that same charming smile on his face.

There was no chance Stanley knew. I'd been careful. 'What do you mean?' I asked, keeping my voice level.

The band began to play a new song, a quiet jazz number, and Stanley stood, ignoring my question. He extended his hand, smiling again as I cocked my head quizzically.

'Dance with me, Roy.'

'What?' I laughed, more out of shock than anything. My heart started to pound, nervous sweat prickled the back of my neck, and I couldn't form a complete sentence. 'Stanley, I don't... I'm not—'

'You don't have to say it. You don't have to say anything. Not tonight. Just dance with me,' he said, his hand still extended.

I looked around, expecting someone to burst through the bushes and catch us together, even though we'd done nothing wrong. I'd rarely even spoken my feelings to myself, let alone to anyone else, but here Stanley was, wanting to dance with me.

I stood slowly, taking his hand. He pulled me against him, his other hand settling on my lower back, and we danced to the music, him smiling and me, wide-eyed and confused.

'Stan, what are we doing?' I whispered, looking into his hazel eyes. 'How hard did you hit the booze before you showed up here?'

'I gotta tell you, Roy,' he murmured, ignoring my question, 'I've wanted to do this for a while. I didn't think you thought of me that way, but we're graduating, so I thought, "What the hell?"'

'You have?' I asked, my breath hitching. I blinked, almost certain now that this was a dream, but the scene didn't change when I opened my eyes again. Stan chuckled, shaking his head slightly.

'I'd tried before, you know. Last Christmas. You remember? We drank all that whiskey and we were afraid Eugene was going to croak.' He laughed, deep and throaty. 'I asked if you wanted to just stay in my room with the rest of the guys, but you insisted on going back to your own bed, so I walked you down the hall to be sure you got there alright. I had a feeling, and I thought I might say something, but I just couldn't do it. Figured it was all in my head when you said goodnight and closed the door in my face.'

'I've learned not to get my hopes up,' I said, looking down. 'It's not exactly common around here.'

Stan took his hand from mine, using it to push my chin up and towards him again, and leaned in, pressing his lips to mine. I stood statue-still for a moment, unsure of what to do, before finally leaning into his kiss. After imagining what it'd be like for so long, it was even better. His lips were soft, the stubble on his chin, cheeks, and upper lip rough from his last shave.

He let go of my face, taking my hand again and swaying once more to the song as if nothing had happened. I sighed, feeling the goofy grin plastered on my face, and leaned my head on his shoulder.

'You sticking around after graduation at all?' he asked quietly.

'For a little, yeah,' I answered.

'Good.'

Not/Coming Out

We didn't talk any more after that, choosing to dance in silence to two more songs, swaying in the shadows of the surrounding thicket. My tie was bunched around my chest, but I didn't care. With my head on his shoulder, me in Stan's arms, the only thing I could see were the polka dots on my tie and the moonbeams illuminating us from above, and it was the best view I'd ever had.

Outings
Katherine Shaw

The first time was on a bus,
surrounded by faces
and teenage chatter,
the hot engine rumbling beneath us.
Public, but safe.
They were my friends,
at least some of them.
One could have been more,
at least, my hormones said so.
I spoke.
An unexpected interruption
and then silence.

The next was in a garden,
a bonfire crackling beside us,
sat under the night sky,
wine coursing through our veins.
You were always so open,
nothing ever held back,
it was about time I returned the favour.
I leaned in, and whispered,
and a weight was lifted.

Not/Coming Out

We were in the car,
sun streamed through the windows
warming my face,
golden fields a blur beside us.
A typical, lazy Saturday afternoon.
You made a joke
and the silence hung forever,
an opening I'd always ignored before,
swallowing down the words.
But it was time. You deserved the truth.
We both did.

I'm standing
in front of so many eyes,
my shaking hands
clutch the words I've prepared.
The lights are blinding,
all the cameras on me,
standing on a precipice
with the wind in my face.
I don't think I'm ready,
but who ever is?
In the endless cycle,
we take a deep breath,
and come out again.

Kaylee in Love
Priscilla Kint

'He sounds amazing, Kaylee.'

We're in her bedroom. She, with her feet dangling off the side of her flower-duvet-covered bed. Me, sitting on her spotted beanbag with a pillow clutched to my chest.

The rosy colour high up on her cheeks brightens. 'I think he might be. But I want to take it slow, you know? It's all still so… fresh.' She rolls her eyes. 'Who knows what could go wrong.'

She says it like a joke, but I see it in her. In the way she raises her shoulders ever so slightly. In the way she blows a loose strand of auburn hair out of her eyes. That careful, considered hesitation.

'Who knows what could go right?' I say.

She plucks at her blanket, gathering Gizmo's grey cat hairs. 'That's true.'

The sun shining through her curtains leaves a pattern of flecks on her baby-pink walls, and I watch them move in the breeze as the smile grows and grows on her face.

*

When I spot the two of them by the school's back door, she's wearing her favourite jeans. High waisted, with stitched details by her thighs. A simple white top paired with them. She fidgets with her golden necklace – the one she got from her grandmother when she turned fifteen – as he wraps an arm around her shoulders.

'A movie, maybe?' Luke proposes. 'Or would you rather do something else?' He gazes at her with this dazzled look in his eyes, as if he's wondering whether he's dreaming or not.

I know the feeling.

She leans into him. With the ivy climbing up the wall behind them and the spring primroses blooming around their feet, they look like they're in a movie. 'I'd kill for a good burger. Can we get burgers?'

Luke nods. He has that perfect bouncy boy hair that, supposedly, every teenager either wants or wants to dig their fingers in.

But she reaches for his hand instead, and squeezes. 'What about mini golf instead of a movie? Then we can actually talk to each other instead of just staring at a boring screen.'

I watch him carefully, wait for his response. This is Kaylee speaking her mind, wholly reasonable in her opinions, even if they go against his.

'You know what? You're right.' His crooked smile and hooded eyes make that blush appear on her cheeks again. 'I have to warn you, though. I am the king of mini golf, so don't expect to be winning.'

Kaylee looks up at him with one raised eyebrow. She has a freckle in the corner by her eye that is so typically hers. 'Challenge accepted, Tiger Woods.'

When she turns to me, her golden smile matches the primroses. 'Do you want to join us?'

I shake my head. 'I'm good. You don't want to arm me with a golf club.'

When Luke laughs, it feels genuine. Still, it's Kaylee's radiance that makes me shine from the inside out. 'But we're still on for our movie night tomorrow, right?' she asks.

I nod. 'Always.'

'Hold on,' Luke says. 'So the two of you can watch a movie, but when we do it, it's staring at a boring screen?'

Kaylee shrugs. 'That's different. That's what best friends do.'

'Do those movie nights include face masks and popcorn and talking about your crushes?'

'Maybe.'

'Hmm.' His eyes narrow playfully. 'I could be persuaded…' His hand trails her shoulder, plays with the edge of her sleeve. In the safe harbour of his arms, she looks like she's never belonged anywhere else.

And my stomach turns.

'You' – Kaylee digs a finger into his chest – 'are not invited.'

His hands go up in defence. 'Okay, okay, message received. Girls' night is holy.'

Not/Coming Out

'You're damn right it is.' Kaylee winks at me, and my stomach settles. 'Don't you forget it.'

He's laughing, and there is that dreamy look again. He has no idea how she's going to change his life. Flip it all the way upside down until he can see a whole new part of the beautiful world he's living in.

*

Two lines of desks in front of me, the whiteboard shows equation after confusing equation. And there are Kaylee and Luke. He's wearing joggers with adidas sneakers – not his usual getup, but he looks comfortable enough. Kaylee's in her strawberry dress, the folds of which she uses to hide the note she's trying to pass to him.

I smile. I know what the note says. A party invitation. To my house. Nothing too big.

Nothing too crazy. Just some people from school and a table full of drinks with red solo cups. I've always wanted to host a party with solo cups.

'Then just do it,' Kaylee told me two days before. 'What's stopping you?'

'Who would show at a party that I throw?' I have a history of short, meaningless relationships and friendships. Small bursts of light that quickly simmer out. Except for Kaylee, of course. Kaylee is a steady sun that keeps on burning.

'Are you kidding me? You're an absolute delight and your house is close enough to the school to be worth it for anyone.' Kaylee grabbed my hand from across the library table. 'Plus, you are an absolute delight.'

I want to pin those words to my bathroom mirror. No, I want to set them as my seven o'clock alarm. So she can tell me every morning. So I can hear those words in her voice for the rest of eternity.

Kaylee hands Luke the note. I watch as his nimble fingers unfold it, as he sends her a kiss, as he gives me a thumbs-up and a wink.

She points at the note, taps her pen. Write it down then.

So he does. Grabs his pencil, circles the Yes, then hands it back. 'Happy, princess?'

'Very much so.'

'Quiet, please,' the teacher says. For a moment, his stylus on the board halts, but then he adds yet another string of meaningless numbers to the board.

*

When Kaylee kisses, it's with purpose. She gives exactly as much of herself as she wants to share. A hand on the back of a neck. Lips parted, but only slightly. Eyes fluttered closed, vulnerable but in complete control.

I shouldn't know all of that. I know I shouldn't. But I do.

It's what I think about before I go to sleep. It's what gets me through the quiet moments of the day. It's like a memory that isn't mine, but gives me strength.

It's everything I want to be when I'm in love. That's all there is to it.

*

It's 11.05 p.m. when Luke's voice cuts through the bass thumping in my crowded living room.

'Kaylee, you're being unreasonable.'

I don't see her, not at first. There's only the music and the group of girls in matching neon outfits dancing in front of me and the faint smell of spilled beer somewhere close.

But then…

'I'm being unreasonable?' They appear out of nowhere. Face to face, shoulders squared, they stare each other down. Her jaw is set. Her eyes shoot fire. Her sequin dress shimmers in the low light, but the room suddenly feels cold. 'All I want is for you to do what you promised me.'

'But the guys—'

'Really, Luke?'

'I—'

'I don't want to hear it.'

'Right.' There's something about his eyes. The way they droop at the corners. The way his tongue folds in on itself when he speaks. 'So you get to push me aside every time something with your friends comes up, but when it's about me and my mates it's a problem and I'm being a pain?'

19

Kaylee's green eyes roll. 'That is not what's going on here.'

He throws his hands up with a grunt. 'I hate it when you're like this.'

A second passes in which she stares at him, her mouth open. I know what she's thinking. I know her by heart. I know that, to her, this sounds too much like a bad sign, too much like approaching danger.

She shakes herself back into action, the lines of her mouth shifting from surprise to determination. 'Well, then go find better!' She turns on her heels – too much fire, too bright – and walks away.

For a moment, I linger on my spot. Watch as Luke's arms slump by his sides. As his beer spills on the carpet – my carpet. 'Wait, are you breaking up with me?'

Kaylee keeps going. She might not have heard, or she might be answering with silence.

'Kaylee, are we breaking up?!'

I leave him where he is. Follow the glittery shimmer of her dress through the crowd. It's silent beyond the music, people staring and awkwardly sipping their solo cups. All here to witness this spectacle. As if it is something to be enjoyed.

I don't call her name. I don't force her to stop. I just wait until she's out the back door in the moonlit garden, where the crickets and the trickle of the fountain in the pond feel louder than ever.

Not/Coming Out

She sits down on the wooden bench by the butterfly bushes and drops her head in her hands.

'What happened?'

'I don't even know.' She doesn't need to lift her head. She knows it's me. That thought fills me up inside.

'It'll be okay,' I say. 'I bet he's just being dumb. Boys can be dumb sometimes. And he's drunk, too.'

I think of more to say. I know that she said some things to Luke that may have been unreasonable and I know there are two sides to every story, but even so I would give anything – anything – to take this hurt away from her right now.

'It'll be fine,' I decide eventually. 'The two of you – you're...' I stop. 'He would be a fool if he lost you.'

'Please,' she whispers. 'Stop.'

My lips seal. The hairs on my arms are standing up.

'I know this isn't the end of the world,' she says, 'but I just need to feel it for a moment. I just need to...' She lifts her face to the star-splattered skies, lets out a grunt. 'I just need to feel bad for a moment.'

'That... That's perfectly fine.'

I wait a beat. The crickets sing around us.

'Is it okay if I stay with you?' I ask her then. 'While you feel bad?'

She nods, and when I sit down, she scoots closer. Puts her head on my shoulder. Sighs, and stills. Almost as if she's come home.

Almost – but not quite.

Not/Coming Out

*

If Kaylee were anything like me, she would throw her phone across the room after hanging up on him. She'd scream with her window open and tell everyone who would listen about the awful person he was. She'd ruin everything they built together in a matter of seconds.

But Kaylee is Kaylee, so instead, we're lying in her double bed and she's clutching her ancient bunny plushie to her chest.

'He just doesn't get it. I don't understand why he can't just…' She lets out a slow breath.

'Do I have to leave him?' she whispers at me beneath the covers. There's a line of spotted mascara underneath her left eye. I wish I could wipe my thumb across it and make it disappear, but it would only smudge further, make more of a mess.

'Do you want to?'

'I don't know.'

I watch a new collection of tears gather, then reach out to touch her hand, the one that's holding on tight to a stuffed bunny ear.

She lets me.

'No,' she says eventually. 'I don't want to break up with him.'

'Then don't,' I tell her.

And I know she won't.

Not/Coming Out

This isn't the end of their story. She'll only break it off when she absolutely has to. But this – this is the moment for communication. For growth. For learning.

She'll reach out, or maybe he'll reach out and say sorry, and he'll handle it with grace, because that's who Luke is. This boy who, despite everything my darkest thoughts might wish for in the middle of the night, is gentle and kind and funny and truly good to her. Who fits her feelings like a favourite sweater.

I reach forward. Brush an auburn streak of hair behind her ear. 'You'll be okay.'

Quietly, she nods. Then she shuts her eyes, releases the bunny, and folds her hands beneath her ear. A tear falls on the pillow, leaving another dark blue smudge. 'I love you, you know that?'

'I do,' I whisper.

She can feel my breath on her face, I'm sure. But I don't let it carry those other words. The ones that feel so powerful and so true when I say them inside my mind.

I'm not ready yet.

There are so many things to think about that I want to be mine for just a moment longer. Like the different shades of her hair in the sunlight and the way her voice changes when she sings her favourite songs in karaoke and how, when I'm around her, I suddenly see so many more colours in the world.

She's here with me, teaching me how to love, but those moments are just for me. Until this sun burns out just a little. Until I no longer crave what she cannot give. Until, perhaps, one day, I'll find a Kaylee that's mine to keep.

But for now, this moment is mine. And it is enough.

The Closet
Breanna Guinta

These four walls hold
dresses and suits,
heels and loafers,
bikinis and trunks,
blue and pink.

I sit on the inside,
with the outside key,
a one way door,
with no way out.

I prefer to be here,
in the locked cage,
not having to explain
gender and sex are
opposing forces.

Here in the closet,
all is comforting.
Why leave when
I can be me?

Not/Coming Out

Unspoken Birdsong
Airic Fenn

Of course I like the name you gave me.
It suits me, and I don't think you could have known just
how much it would reflect my identity.
To reject it would be a betrayal of me.
But to say there isn't a level of satisfaction I feel when I
employ my *nom de plume* beyond the page would be a
lie.

> *Fulfilling my namesake*
> *I am a corvid,*
> *a bird,*
> *a faerie,*
> *gathering more for my collection.*

Of course, I can't tell you that.

I can't tell you that in my circles I party with she/theys
and ve/vyms.
That I myself prefer they/them.

(When I tried, you used it as a punchline a month later

Not/Coming Out

But maybe that's okay.
Of course, I want you to understand.
But understanding is hard,
and coming out is harder.

So, I still let you call me *your little girl.*
In the spirit of things, a part of me always will be.

Of course, if you'd listened to my tune, you would know
your little girl never became a woman.
Never wanted to.

> ('Woman' always left me with worms in my gut
> and a strange taste on my lips when sung aloud.)

I wish I could tell you how euphoric that child felt when
their teammates tried to insult them.
Said they sounded like a boy.

Of course, when told, you responded, 'no you don't.'

> (But I did, until all the voices of the boys around me
> settled into smooth tenors, leaving mine behind to
> forever sound like that unfledged child).

But I can't tell you that. And maybe that's okay.

27

Not/Coming Out

I didn't have to come out to my friends.
It was a slow reveal, like a well-told story
with plenty of crumbs for the reader to peck at along the
way.
It was a reveal over countless songs
about life,
about school,
about crushes,
about not-quite-but-something-like crushes.
By the time I found my voice, no one was surprised.

'That's fitting for you.
You've always had the vibe of a genderless fae creature.'

It was easy.

I came out to the rest of the world online, just for good
measure.
That was easy, too.
Ironically, you didn't see me spread my wings.
Even though it was directed at you.

Of course, you won't hear this song, either. At least not
yet.
And maybe that's okay, too.

— ▮▮▮▮▮▮

Not/Coming Out

Stereotypes
Samantha Maich

CW: suicide mention

Are you... you know?
Are you so audacious,
As to think that you are owed
Any explanation of my truth
To satisfy a fleeting curiosity?
Are you so cowardly,
As to make this demand,
Without being able
To say gay?

He likes girly things.
He likes both makeup and sci-fi movies,
And making delicious tomato basil soup
To share with his friends,
Gathered together on a cold day.
He likes knowing
That who he is attracted to
Is the least interesting part of him,
To those whose opinions matter.

Not/Coming Out

She wants attention.
She wants to live in a town
Where she can hold hands with her girlfriend,
Without the predatory stares of men
Oozing over their palms.
She wants to bring her love
To her family holiday celebration,
Without stilted conversations
And averted gazes.

You must be mentally ill.
You must feel so confined,
Living in a world
That punishes differences
With pointed accusations.
You must feel so angry,
Knowing that you hold yourself back,
Afraid of becoming the target
Instead of the arrow.

They're trying to convert our children.
They're trying to be
The person they wish they had
When they were children
Wrestling against a society that diminished them.
They're trying to show
That things get better
Because validation

Not/Coming Out

Is suicide prevention.

I love you
Samantha Maich

CW: anxiety

Anxiety fills my stomach
Swirling ocean waves
Crashing against ships
That hold hope and dread

Nauseously descending stairs
Thud thud thud
My heart matches my footsteps
As I walk towards my future

Palms sweating
Mouth dry
The liquid of my body
Isn't where it should be

Scalp tingling
Eyes prickling
Shallow breathing
I enter the room

Not/Coming Out

A sense of dread
I spy you at our table
If I trust you so much
Why is this so hard?

You look up with a smile
A line forms between your eyebrows
You know something is happening
And reach out to me

I sit down
Ears pounding with blood
A pivotal moment
I will my courage to build

You reach over
And hold my hand
A dam breaks
And words burst forth

I think I'm a girl
Frozen in time
My truth has escaped
From the safety of my vessel
Vulnerability is left in its place

A second passes

Not/Coming Out

I meet your eyes
You stand up
And wrap me in your arms

That's okay
Thank you for trusting me
I support you
I love you

3 In 4
Robyn Hill

CW: anxiety

Clinking of cups and screeches from kettles and scraping of chairs and people-people-people-so-many-people-bustling-past-repeating-their-names-and-spellings-catching-up-with-old-friends-laughing-too-loud-talking-too-loud-existing-too-loud—

I bet none of them were about to cry.

A lull in the conversation brought me back. I tried to wiggle in my seat but my legs stayed welded to the leather. My bare thighs sucked onto the seat like aggressive oysters, barnacles that refused to be chiselled off. Who knew thighs could sweat so much in January?

'So basically, I wanted to tell you both something,' she started. She *started.* Why was I even here? I never thought I was the type to cave to peer pressure but I guess when it's your girlfriend it's not really peer pressure. Right?

Opposite us, our two friends leaned forward, interested. This sounded like more than gossip, but something *serious.* They clutched their obnoxious drinks, one with far too much whipped cream for someone who claims to be lactose intolerant, the other with far too much coffee for a fifteen-year-old.

'Um, so, I'm bi,' she said, just like that. *Oh gosh.* Is that my cue to go? How did she just *say* that? If I haven't even said it to myself yet, how do I convey it with conviction to people I care about? How do you form the words in your mouth and not choke on them? How did they not curdle in her throat, blocking every sound?

'Oh, nice. Me too.'

The voice came from my friend opposite me. *What?* The four of us looked at ourselves and each other, tumbling into laughter and shock. Maybe if-I-spoke-quick-enough-whilst-they-were-laughing-I-could-get-it-out-and-they-wouldn't-notice—

'Me too.'

'Wait really?'

'You're joking right?'

'No, I'm actually—'

I lowered my voice like a child about to say the f word,

'*gay,*   but yeah.'

Out in the open, I was out. And that was that. Except for

My mum

37

Not/Coming Out

My sister
My dad
My other friends
My other family
Strangers in the street

Myself.

Listening to my gurgling gut and knowing it wasn't upset by my overpriced drink, I could feel this was wrong. But maybe it wasn't so much of a "coming out of the closet" as much as a "getting the ball rolling". I had, albeit not confidently, hurled myself into a human-hamster-ball-zorb and bounced down a big metaphorical hill. As my friends and girlfriend giggled around me, delving into why Ruby Rose was "hot" rather than "pretty", I knew this was just the start. This hill was steep, and whether I liked it or not, I was picking up speed.

Your Man
Emily Byars

There are plenty of gays in Texas. Texas is where all the Alabama gays move to come out without getting disowned. So yeah, theoretically growing up near Dallas I should have been fine, except for a couple of tiny details: my mother was born-and-raised Southern Baptist, and my father was a duke – of the Hazzard variety. Coming out to them would be like asking for permission to go to conversion therapy.

Because of this, I wasn't the gay you might want me to be – I never got caught wearing my mother's lipstick or lip-synching to Madonna or whatever The Gays™ are supposed to do. I never did quite fit in with my dad's drinking buddies or anything, but I had a couple of girlfriends in middle school and even taught a children's Sunday school class for a couple of years. (I have this conspiracy theory, actually, that all Southern gay men work in a church as a way to avoid being sent to hell by Mrs. Carol Ann in the fourth pew on the right.)

It had been easy to hide this part of myself from everyone, so easy that I sometimes doubted it existed. Maybe I'm bisexual. Maybe I'm asexual. Maybe I'm too young to know, and all teenagers are just swimming through this sea of identity and sex with floaties on each arm, kicking around violently until someone finds them who can help them learn to swim. I decided to just float around, and that seemed to work for eighteen years. I never actively pursued anyone, no one actively pursued me. But love is as passive as it is powerful, and I found myself in over my head.

In the month of June, I both graduated high school and turned eighteen, and my parents finally got me a car. It was a brand-new – just kidding, it was mom's old Tahoe that she bought when I was in third grade. Still, it was better than nothing. It was independence, and I was feeling particularly grown up. Our senior class president was having a big graduation party, and I had convinced mom to let me go, and, more importantly, to let me go by myself. I dressed in the pseudo-frat-boy fashion I thought would be appropriate and prayed that this would go well. See, I had never been the pseudo-frat-boy type, which meant I had never had more than two friends at a time, which meant it was incredibly likely that I was about to spend the next three hours standing by the food table talking to somebody's mom about what I was going to major in next fall.

And this was true, at least for a while. Mrs. Greene – who insisted I call her Mrs. Sharon – asked me all about everything I've been asked a thousand times – was I going to school, where was I going, what was I majoring in, would I be staying in a dorm, was I getting scholarships, would I be working, the list goes on and on. If you've ever been a senior in high school, you know exactly what I mean. My mouth somehow replied as if on autopilot, but my eyes were elsewhere.

A guy had come up to the table and grabbed some food, nothing out of the ordinary there. But then he just hung around, clearly wanting to interject but too polite to do so. I know it sounds completely unsexy when I tell it to you now, but for me, to see that a stranger appeared to be seeking out my company was absolutely unheard-of. His eyes all but begged mine to meet his charming gaze, which I, of course, avoided like the plague. But I managed to escape Mrs. Greene's interrogation, excusing myself to eat my wings and assuming - no - hoping, maybe even praying, that he would follow.

'Hey man. Saul,' he said, extending his hand, a smile crinkling up his face.

'Nathan. So what – uh, I mean, who—' How do you ask somebody why they're at a party without sounding like an ignorant douche?

'I'm one of Alyssa's friends. Honestly I'm surprised Mrs. Sharon didn't introduce us.' Alyssa was Mrs. Greene's oldest daughter, about to go back to A&M majoring in something-or-other – she told me, but that was in the part of the conversation I had zoned out for.

So, you know how in the movies it's like boy-meets-girl and the world just absolutely stops? Yeah, it wasn't really like that. We ate, we made small talk, we exchanged numbers. And for that day, that was it. But that was enough.

I can't describe it to you in any way that doesn't sound stupid, but it was like I finally understood the concept of attraction – I literally felt like I had a magnet in my stomach, like it had been there my whole life, but I had only just found anyone with the opposite pole. Saul Arellano: I went over every detail over and over – his dark, slicked back hair, his perfect teeth, his smile that took up two-thirds of his face. His muscular build was canceled out by his baby face and somewhat short stature. And his eyes – God, I wish it wasn't the eyes, it's so cliché. But it was – he had this way of looking at you that would make you feel safe and smart and irresistibly attractive all at once. He messaged me the next night, though it felt like seven years, and we stayed up until four a.m. talking about nothing. It was perfect. No one had ever listened to me like that.

*

We didn't really have a first date. We met up at the park, then at the burger place across from the school, then at the pool. Nowhere really date-y. So I can't really tell you when we started dating, but I can tell you when I had my first kiss. It was June twenty-first, the day of the summer solstice. Appropriate, as it certainly felt like one of the longest days of my life. Saul picked me up at nine o'clock that morning, and we drove around forever. We stopped

42

for lunch at some diner connected to a gas station just across the state line into Oklahoma. It was mediocre at best – the fries were soggy and the soda was watered down. The burger was fine, but it would've been a lot better without the flies.

We kept driving, ending up in some random park. Not like a national park, with trees or whatever. Like a park park – a walk-the-dog-and-watch-the-kids park.

'This is where we're going?' I asked, not disappointed but far from enthusiastic.

'I mean, not if you don't want to. I thought it'd be fun.'

'I mean, sure. Swings?'

'Race ya!' He bolted off, nearly crashing into a little girl and her mom.

We got to the swing set at almost the same time (he would tell you that he won. He lies). It had been a long time since I had swung, so I hadn't anticipated just how much my feet would drag in the sand.

'What did you do on the playground? Were you a swinger or a slider?'

'Both, I guess. I just wanted to be high.'

'In elementary school?!' He grinned.

'No, I mean, guess I just always wanted to be up, away from everybody. Like a bird.'

Saul got up suddenly from his swing. 'Here,' he said, giving me a solid push, then another. I lifted my feet off the ground, allowing myself to be swept up in the moment. I was reminded how it felt to tap the tree

43

branches with your toes, to go so high the swing almost flips, the feeling of the little sand grains getting impossibly stuck inside your sock between your toes and of how difficult it is to return back to the ground when you're done.

'I've got a better idea!' he said, taking my hand and sprinting across the playground (the former was, of its own accord, enough to make my heart jump, as I hadn't even had my hand held up to this point – pathetic, I know). Saul scaled the jungle gym, beckoning to me as he stood atop it, chin up, hands on his hips, like an explorer overlooking his newly claimed dominion.

I scrambled to the top (albeit with far less finesse) and matched his gallant pose. 'What shall we do now, my brave comrade?' he bellowed in my direction.

'Whatever you like,' I countered with a coquettish smirk. The silly moment turned serious as he brought his hand to my cheek.

'Is this okay?'

I leaned in, implying the affirmative, and just like that we kissed. Nothing serious, nothing more than a peck really. It was awkward, as most first kisses (especially first first kisses) tend to be – we were still standing, still balancing on top of the jungle gym – but it was somehow fitting. After a moment of uncomfortable perfection, I finally muttered, 'I think we should sit.'

'Uh, yeah.' We fumbled around, trying to bend ourselves up to sit – then kiss – without falling. Somehow it worked, and somehow no one's little kid snitched on us, because somehow we made out on top of the jungle gym. And it was awesome. Still awkward, hands and tongues desperately finding their way. But awesome, nonetheless.

*

We got back in his car, a little flustered, a LOT hungry, and ready to get out of Oklahoma. He was the first to finally speak.

'So, this may be implied, but...' He was clearly nervous. It was adorable. 'Would you want to be, like, my official boyfriend?'

'That depends. Would you want to be, like, my official boyfriend?'

'Oh, shut up," he said with a smile. 'I guess that means yes?'

'Yes, that means yes!'

He pulled into my driveway and attempted to kiss me goodnight. I pulled away anxiously.

'What's wrong?'

'My parents don't know.'

'About us?'

'About me. About any of it. Like, they're not cool with it.'

'Have you tried to talk to them about it?'

'Jesus, are you insane? No, they'd kill me!'

'Well maybe if I—'

'No, it's fine, just go on home. I'll text you later.' I got out, slamming the door harder than I intended. Saul opened his.

'Nathan, can't I at least come in and—'

'No. Look, I'm sorry. Maybe some other time.'

Saul shoved his hands deep in his pockets, his eyes locked on mine. There was nothing more he could say, just a disappointed sigh as he got back in his car. I watched his tail-lights until I couldn't see them anymore.

I spent the rest of the night alone and extremely confused, caught between the euphoria of the playground and the anxious frustration of my driveway. I tried to message Saul. He tried to message back. It was awkward, but this time not so awesome.

*

A few days went by, and he, almost out of the blue, texted to ask if I wanted to come over to his house for supper on Friday.

'With your parents?' I texted back, more than a little nervous.

He sent back a series of texts in quick succession:

'Yeah. I told them about you, and they're really excited to meet you!'

'We're having tacos.'

'Get it, 'cause we're Mexican?' (this one had a laughing emoji).

'Anyway, they said your parents were welcome to come too, but I told them I didn't think they'd want to'

46

Not/Coming Out

I was overwhelmed… at best. We hadn't even seen each other since the park and everything, and he wanted me to meet his parents? I hadn't been convinced that he even still wanted to be with me, much less this. But some devil on my shoulder must've gotten custody of my phone, because I found myself typing, 'Sure, just tell me what time and I'll clear it with mom.'

*

I know I've used the words 'nervous' and 'awkward' pretty liberally so far, but I can't even come up with a word strong enough to describe the way I felt Friday. I put on jeans and a t-shirt, then a button-down, then slacks and a tie, then I stripped back to my boxers and just stared for a while, waiting for the sweat to dry. I tried again: deodorant, undershirt, okay… I decided to strike it up the middle, just my nicer jeans and a button-down. I was already sweating again. In my defense, it was nearly July.

His parents were perfect. His house was perfect. His baby sister Ana was annoying – and, in her way, perfect. They all ushered me in and smothered me with hugs, asking me what they could get me to drink before I even had a chance to sit down.

'So how did you two meet?' his dad asked, bringing us bottles of water.

His mom chimed in right behind. 'Yeah, we wanna know everything! Who asked out who, how did it happen?!'

Not/Coming Out

It felt like I was in the twilight zone. It was too normal. They asked all those kinds of questions that you ask your son when he brings home a girl. I am lots of things, but I'm no girl. It was like they didn't notice. Even Ana, who was all of maybe eight, got right in his face to 'whisper' to him, 'Did ya kiss him yet?' She made a grossed-out face, but it was obvious she was more curious than anything.

We answered every question one by one and demolished more than our fair share of tacos (I spilled salsa on my favorite shirt). On one hand, I was elated to be so accepted by his family, but on the other, it stung. This was the reality I could never have.

Instead, I'd gathered from whispers that mom's cousin Carla didn't show her face at the reunions anymore after the one year she dared to bring her "friend" with her. I'd watched dad change the channel in disgust when Glee came on T.V. I'd listened to sermons about not only the sanctity of marriage between a man and a woman but the abomination of men who lie with men, all met with resounding nods and amens from a congregation of people who claimed to love me. From my own mother.

Mrs. Arellano took my dirty dishes to the sink. I wanted to cry.

'Well,' I said, trying to hide my emotions and make my great escape, 'it's getting a little late, and my parents will want me home soon.'

Not/Coming Out

'Oh, it's only nine o'clock, are you sure you can't stay another half hour or so?' his father asked. It meant a lot that he would offer, but I just couldn't do it.

'I wish I could. Thank you for everything!'

And with that, I left the Arellano house. Saul walked me to my car and, as usual, saw through my nonsense.

'Okay, cut the bullshit, what's wrong?'

'I mean, I'm glad your parents like me and everything, they were incredible, but—'

'Your parents?'

I nodded. 'It's not fair. I wish I could give you that kind of welcome. I wish I could let you just saunter through the door and that I could just say, "Mom, Pop, this is my lover Saul. We are very happy and we are here to eat tacos." Do you know how wonderful that would be?'

'Lover?' He raised a single eyebrow.

'You know what I mean.'

'I know, and I really do hate that whole situation for you,' he said, shaking his head. 'I know you don't think so, but you may need to have a conversation. Maybe just with your mom, she seems nice from everything you've told me. She might take it better than you think. A lot of parents do.'

'Maybe. I'll think about it.' I wasn't gonna think about it. I had already thought about it and had swiftly come to the conclusion that my parents were not the sort that would ever be accepting of something like that. Maybe they wouldn't kick me out, but they certainly would never let me feel comfortable in my own skin. Some things are just better left unsaid.

'Well, you just get home safe.'

'Okay, I'll text when I get there.'

'Oh, hey.'

'Yeah?'

'I love you.' Of all the things I had expected him to say, that was not one of them. I took a breath, smiled, and – can you believe it? – I said it back.

'I love you too. And tell your parents I said thanks again and it was a pleasure meeting them.'

*

I didn't recover for days. I had this perpetual half-smile. I ate nothing but strawberries and macaroni-and-cheese. I'm glad it was summer, because schoolwork would've been impossible. My dad was, ironically, convinced I had fallen in love.

'That Paul boy must have an awfully good-looking sister, son,' he said, taking a long swig of his beer. 'Anything you want to tell me?'

My heart thudded. 'No, sir.'

'Not even a name?'

'No, sir. I mean yes, sir. Um—'

'I'm just yanking your chain. You don't have to tell me nothing. But I tell you what, whoever this little viper is, if you hurt her I'll get the shotgun after your ass myself, you hear me?'

'Yes, sir.'

'Her family Christian?' Even though dad wasn't much of a church-going man himself those days (much to my mother's chagrin), there was only one right answer to this question.

'I'm not sure,' I said, telling the truth where I still could. Saul and all his beautiful, nosey family ran through my mind. 'They seem to be good people though, so probably.'

'That's good, son; that's important. You want a drink?' he said, as he finished his beer and reached for another.

'I'm eighteen.' Now I know normally kids have their first drink far before twenty-one, but normal kids haven't dealt with my mom.

'Right, you're eighteen, kid, all but grown. Got yourself a girl, might as well have yourself a beer. You'll need one before too much longer, trust me.'

'I'm good.'

'Suit yourself. If God didn't intend for us to have a few beers then why the hell'd he put them in a six-pack, dammit?'

I didn't argue with dad's, let's call it interesting, logic. I just went to my room and headed to bed.

*

A few weeks later, I picked Saul up from his house for an ice cream date, blaring country music. Now I know that this is also not in alignment with the Gay Agenda, but I grew up listening to it and sometimes your childhood just sticks around in places that maybe it shouldn't.

'The fuck is this?' Saul said, getting in the car with a look of suspicious amusement.

'The fuck does it sound like?'

'I mean I know what, but, like, why?'

'One word: basses. Have you heard Josh Turner sing?' It's true – country music has always had and always will have the market cornered for sexy, deep voices. It's a shame they also have the market cornered for homophobic fans.

'Do you plan on coming out to your parents any time soon?' He had changed the topic faster than I was prepared to talk about it. I shut down.

'Dude. Stop.'

'I'm sorry, babe, I just—'

'I thought we already had this conversation. I said I'd think about it. Look I don't care if it's pride month or whatever the fuck. My parents aren't going to be proud of this.'

'Pride month was last month. But that's literally not the point. Don't you think they already know?'

'My dad is literally clueless. He just gave me a hopelessly heterosexual sex talk last week.'

'You just got the sex talk? What are you, twelve?'

I'll admit, that hit a little too close to home. I knew he had the upper hand here since he had been in one or two relationships before, and honestly, I hadn't ever really had a proper sex talk – my school didn't offer it and mom was an abstinence-only kind of woman. To this day I don't think she would even say the word 'masturbate' out loud. Regardless, the so-called sex talk dad had given me was enough to keep me in the closet for another five-to-seven business years.

'Not the birds-and-the-bees sex talk. The,' I cleared my throat, prepared to give my best impersonation of my dad's drawl. 'Alright now, son. I'm dumb but I ain't stupid, and I know now you got yourself a gal. Now y'all might start getting frisky, or at least thinking on it real hard, so you at least should know about three things: condoms, the clitoris, and reverse cowgirl. Don't tell your mama I told you none of this.'

For once, Saul was the one who seemed awkward. He was genuinely at a complete loss for words. I had been too. Finally, he stammered, 'What the actual fuck? What did you even say?'

'I mean, the typical response to a kid having that kind of talk with their parents is extreme awkwardness, so it was easy to play it off. I just sort of nodded and avoided eye contact.'

'So the same thing you always do when your dad talks to you.' It was a statement, not a question. And I hated that he was right.

'I guess. Hey, are we getting ice cream or what?'

'Yeah, but before we do, I've got something to tell you.'

'Okay, shoot.'

'I called your mom earlier. I'm coming to dinner tonight.'

'I'm sorry, you did what?' I couldn't tell if the tension in my jaw was from nerves or anger or both.

Saul put on his customer service voice. 'Hi, is this Nathan's mom? Yes ma'am, this is his friend Saul. I'm good, how are you? Good. Nathan and I were just wondering if it would be okay if I stayed over at his house tonight. Yes ma'am, spaghetti sounds wonderful, I'll see you later. Bye-bye.'

'A sleepover? What the hell is wrong with you, Saul?'

'Just helping out a friend. If she already likes me, she can't be that mad at me if-slash-when she finds out.'

'You underestimate my family's hypocrisy; I hope you're aware of that.'

'You know, you keep saying that. I just want to find out for myself. Have a little spaghetti, build a pillow fort, have a good time.'

'If you say so.' I wasn't sure, but I guessed there was nothing on the surface wrong with two dudes playing video games until two a.m.

*

I was thankful but angry. My parents were just as perfect as his had been. My dad gave 'Paul' a solid handshake and a 'That's a good Christian name you got there, boy.' My mom was all smiles, serving up the spaghetti and garlic bread just as we walked through the doorway. She asked about his parents and whether he was working anywhere.

It was like one of those carnival mirrors, the same yet distorted.

We went to my room after supper. 'I hope you know I was serious about the pillow fort,' Saul said.

'Oh, I know. I already got all the extra ones from mom and dad's room. So I vote pillow fort and video games: FIFA or NCAA?'

'FIFA, duh.'

'Oh, right. Mexican.' I could never quite tell if Saul was actually proud of his heritage or if he just made fun of himself so no one else could. I was the only one he ever allowed to make Mexican jokes about him, so I'm guessing the latter.

We had a pillow fight amid the building of our fortress, then hooked up the game. Somewhere in the middle of the first half, though, we got distracted. I could make some joke here about 'scoring' and 'playing for the other team' or whatever, but the truth of the matter is this: if you believe in virginity, I lost mine that night. It was wonderful. It was unprotected. It was nerve-wracking – my door was unlocked the whole time. I felt like I was desecrating a temple, but I had neither the desire nor the will to stop.

*

We got up the next morning and ate breakfast as though we had, in fact, stayed up too late playing FIFA.

'Yeah, he kicked my ass,' I told my dad.

55

'That's fine, kid,' he said, looking over at Saul. 'But if you ever wanna play some real football I'll hand yours to ya on a platter.'

'Yes sir, that's a deal.' He was more natural talking with my dad than I was. I wasn't sure if that made me jealous or proud.

I had driven him to my house, so his dad came to get him the next morning. My family all walked him to the door, wanting, of course, to meet his family. On his way out, Saul kissed me. It wasn't even particularly passionate, just long enough to be seen. 'I love you.' My stomach was in my throat. I felt betrayed.

I said nothing in return. My parents no longer wanted to meet his. His dad waved. Mom slammed the door, sobbing her way back into the house. I followed her to their bedroom. Another slamming door. She just needs time, I thought. I hoped.

I circled around the house like a puppy, trying to figure out what in God's name to do next. I couldn't go back to my room, back to the fort. Couldn't go back to my car. Every space held the memory of a man I loved but didn't know.

After a few brief moments, which for all I knew could have been hours, dad came back inside.

'Wanna watch the game, son?' he asked, easing back into his recliner.

'Sure.'

Not/Coming Out

I sat uncomfortably on the couch, staring at the TV. Not watching, just staring. I tried to come up with something, anything.

'He's Mexican. His whole family is like that. They're affectionate.' It was a lie that could've been true. I prayed it would take.

He bent the tab back and forth on his can of beer until it fell in. I kept staring, my eyes somehow dried out and watery. A commercial for Doritos. A commercial for Claritin. Some sports commentator I'm supposed to have heard of.

He spat tobacco into an old orange juice bottle. 'You weren't gonna tell me.'

'I didn't think you'd understand.'

'I don't.'

Aside from the game, all was uncomfortably quiet again. I turned my gaze toward the window as though I had never seen curtains before. Dad got up from his chair with a grunt, heading back into the kitchen. The familiar sound of the fridge door opening, a beer can sliding out, the fridge door closing again. The magnet from Dollywood fell off with a gentle thud, so dad, like always, put it back.

'Here, son. I told you you'd be needing one.' He placed the can on the coffee table and sat down beside me on the couch.

The Gates
Sarah Fletchins

CW: gatekeeping

I'm proud, but that doesn't mean
I want to tell you.
I have a theory, you see,
that the old, time-worn rusty keys
I've kept won't really let me in.

They're like everything else in the attic
and the stale, sitting dust of the cellar:
They had an expiration date.
Unprinted, unspoken, but not so secret.

They had conditions, clauses I have broken,
and now that door could creak open
to a welcoming roar,
or be jammed slick stuck with sticky threads;
the cobwebs that toxic spiders spin.

Either way, it's all too much for me –
a risk not worth the wrath.
So the simplest things suffice.

Not/Coming Out

A blanket to wrap my colours in,
a peaceful place to watch
the rest revel.

My Pride
is inside and theirs
is out

But, I exist.
That just doesn't mean
that I want to have to tell you.

Baby Steps
Sky DuVall

CW: gender dysphoria

'I'm not trans,' I say as I scroll through the news.

I can't be. Surgery sounds scary, and the world would want to kill me. I'm fine just the way I am. I think I could even be happy, if I keep trying hard enough.

'I'm not trans,' I mutter, pulling up another pair of men's pants in the women's changing room. My hair creates a curtain around me, sticking to my neck and face. I resist the urge to yank it off my head.

I'm nervous, my breath coming in quick, tepid huffs. It feels taboo to be trying on men's clothes and everything feels too fast. A creeping sense that at any moment, someone will open the door and scowl that I don't belong. But these pants fit way better on my body, and I'm loving the way they look.

I love the shirts too. Thick stripes and dark, solid colors that always match. The way the dense fabric feels against my skin. I love how boxy it is, nothing clinging to my curves and showing off my body. It just hangs, naturally.

Not/Coming Out

'I'm not really anything like that,' I say. My friend and I are exploring the LGBTQIA+ Center at college and I feel an odd sense of belonging here. 'I'm just an ally, that's all. I hope I'm not intruding.'

I really didn't want to come, but it surprises me how easy it is to be around everyone. I relate to people's stories and connect to them on a deeper level. A connection I haven't really found with other people. I feel safe and content. I exchange my number with a few people. Still, I'm just an ally.

'I'm not trans,' I whisper, mostly to myself, as the hairdresser cuts off my hair. Large slivers of hair fall to the floor like snakes, becoming a pile of brown silk below my feet. I have immaculate hair. It's soft and shiny and the people around me gasp as they watch chunks of it fall to the floor. It feels liberating to me, but the glances and whispers are starting to make me feel nervous.

The hairdresser brings the razor out and starts buzzing down my hair in the back. I feel euphoria from the blade cutting so close. This is how my hair was always meant to be cut.

She hands me a mirror to take a look at my short hair, holding her breath nervously at my hairstyle choice, and letting it out as I smile. I can see myself for the first time in the mirror. All the mismatched pieces of my face come together to create me in the reflection, and it's strange to actually see yourself for the first time. Years of looking at a fragmented view, only to have it all come together by a haircut.

'I'm really not,' I mumble out, chewing on the straw of the iced tea in my hand.

I watch as two men hold hands. I feel this deep sadness come over me as I realize I want that, more than anything. To just hold hands with another man, as a—

'I'm not trans,' I almost shout, as a coworker asks me my pronouns. 'But like, maybe, you could use they/them? And I've been thinking about changing my name. Something more gender neutral. But that's it, because I'm not trans.'

I'm just exploring, and that's it. There's nothing wrong with trying something new. It doesn't change the years I've invested in that one gender I was pushed into at birth. Nothing has to change, not really.

I'm not ready for things to change. Not now.

'Ummm, can I ask you a question?' a customer says, looking up at me with curiosity and excitement. A teenager, the same age I was when I started pushing down certain thoughts. The same age I knew I was too scared to even take a peek at the truth. The same age I turned my back on myself, only to regret every second of it now.

'Sure,' I say. 'Go ahead.'

'Are you trans?'

I almost let the same answer slip out of my mouth. The one I've conditioned myself to give every time I, or anyone else, question my gender. But instead I pause, wondering what it would have been like to actually see another trans person when I was a child. When I was telling everyone that I was, in fact, a boy, how could they not see that?

If I had met a trans person or knew more about it, how would my life be different now?

'More questioning, but I think so,' I say, smiling down at this person. It feels weird to admit it aloud, and the anxiety is still there. But it melts away as this teenager lets out a sigh of relief.

'Is it really scary? I don't think I'm ready.'

'No, it's not that scary. You don't have to do anything you don't want to. You can start with baby steps. And yeah, the world is scary, but, you'll find a community of people who will support and respect you for who you are. And I think that's worth the world.'

Maybe I am trans, and I get to have the life I want. And maybe getting to live that life isn't as scary as I always thought. I know it's going to take a while before it all makes sense, but that's okay. I can take another step when I'm ready.

A For Effort

A. Lynn Rosefinch

CW: gender dysphoria

I want to be someone else, because I can't want as myself.

I can't imagine my body stripped bare for another without shame clinging to every limb like poison ivy.

Being touched, being loved; *that* I crave. Gentle fingertips brushing over my thigh, a soft hand tracing the knots in my spine, the feeling of being a precious thing to be cared for and cherished, that is what I long for in my lonely nights.

But when I yearn for sex, I yearn as a stranger. I watch from a distance as faceless characters act out their fantasies – *my fantasies?* In my feverish dreams I am a third-person narrator, omniscient and unknown. Invisible. Able to be forgotten about, a fourth wall I don't want to break.

Many envy attractive celebrities or fictional characters living their happily-ever-afters, and so do I. I am jealous of their temptation, of their desire. I want the body and the brain of someone who wants and who is wanted.

I wish my body sparked to life at hushed whispers of illicit promises.

I wish my hands ached for a body to explore.

I wish I could exist in my fantasies without killing the mood.

The pain of wanting to want is intense and debilitating. It's a baby bird living in the hollow nest of my chest, eating the words I've swallowed over and over again. I feel empty, like a higher power ran out of a vital ingredient during my creation but shrugged their shoulders and said 'it'll probably be fine.'

And more than anything, I want it to be fine.

I want the guilt in my gut to pass through; to stop feeling like my body is a bargaining chip to keep my partner from leaving.

I want the fear to fade; to stop wondering if life would be easier if my anxiety didn't keep me at arm's length.

I want to be okay with wanting from a distance.

ae·go·sex·u·al

A disconnect between the self and the object of sexual arousal.

Sexual attraction without self.

Maybe saying the word will help me. Maybe embracing a label so niche will help convince my mind that yes, I am okay. Maybe breaking the shame of the word itself will help peel back each layer of shame encompassing me.

Or maybe it'll do nothing, and I'll spend my days wanting a desire I can't manifest, and maybe it'll hurt until the day I die.

Might as well try.

I am aegosexual. And I am okay.

Over and Over
Hannah Rose

CW: erasure

Coming out is a weird one. We talk about "coming out" like it's a one-time thing. You're in the closet, then you're out, and that's it. Once and done.

But that's never what it really is. You come out over and over and over again.

You come out to yourself. A tiny voice in the back of your mind whispers 'actually when you say you think she's pretty, you're kind of saying more than that'.

You come out to your friends. Kind of sort of, but not really, when you're drunk and you kiss them and it's all fun and games. Except to you, who actually felt something flutter deep in your tummy.

You come out to your other friends. Seriously, for real, you tell them that you find both girls and boys attractive. Some of them don't care, but one might tell you that they'd rather you weren't gay in front of them.

You come out to your boyfriend. He thinks it's hot, acts like girls only like other girls for the male gaze. He removes the goodness.

Not/Coming Out

You come out to a girl you like. You look into those warm brown eyes and you stutter and you hold hands and you try to kiss each other but you mess up and bump heads. And the kiss is more than it ever has been with anyone else.

You come out to your mum. She's cool with you being in a relationship with a girl and believes that yeah you might like her as more than a friend, but you're not gay. Not really. It's just one of those things.

You come out to a guy you've just started seeing. He's uncomfortable. He thinks you'll leave him for a girl. You couldn't possibly be faithful.

You come out to your friends. You make new friends. You have to come out again. You make new friends. You have to come out again. You make new friends. You have to come out again.

You come out over and over and over.

Bullies
Brandon Shane

I don't want to tell my family that you're only a friend,
someone I confide in about my love for others
rather than the object of my passions, dreams,
& as the cis boys & cis girls watch their movies,
hold hands in public squares without glares,
our shoulders are not even allowed a brush,
& like fires smiles are rapidly extinguished,
by forces dedicated to their erasure.
We are a pendulum caught in an endless swing,
between hiding our love & being enveloped,
finding the crooks & crevices where we can
escape from their all-seeing eye that hunts,
our safe havens & hideouts pillaged in raids;
boys on the run again. For the grave
crime of being a man who loves another man,
stuck in the traditions of my parents, yours,
expectations that wage war against our nature,
as adults we are still treated as children,
afraid of what our colleagues will say,
as if we are still on the playground,
frightened by the reactions of neighbors,
distant relatives who haven't spoken to us

Not/Coming Out

in years, but would chime the moment
our sexuality became clear. Take my hand,
& let us walk to a pier's edge, gaze at the
horizon, down to abyssal rock, where there
is only absence. 'We're no different.'
you tell me; all we do is hide underneath
a shallow surface, our complexities unseen,
storms swallowed & raging within.

Gradually Spellcasting in the Snow
Daniel Skentelbery

I am here to find the labels. No. Labels is the wrong word. I'm here to find a language. This is a quest to find a spelling.

In the depths of a snow-covered forest, flyers for 'Prom 2014' travel through the cool breeze, and one hits me as I'm skipping across the stepping stones of a frozen stream.

I didn't go; vocal pressure pushed me away, and I stayed at home listening to podcasts and painting. Three months later, I did not go to the Fresher's Welcome Party. Instead, I sought like-minded people at the Fresher's Film Night, but I left when no one else arrived.

At university, I feared that I had missed out. Uni was a seven-year panic.

'Excuse me, take your foot off me.'

I look down at the stepping stone under my foot.

'Oh, of course,' I say apologetically and jump to the other side of the stream. 'If you don't mind me asking,' I say, turning back to the stone, 'have you ever been in love?'

'There was a girl in my physics class,' the stone answers. 'She struggled, so I helped her. In the end, we

71

worked well as lab pairs. Though her friends would tease her, say that we were a couple.'

'Me too. She would turn bright red denying it.'

'Sometimes I desire romantic companionship,' says the stepping stone.

'Me too. Though only in theory.'

I thank the stone for their time and walk on.

There is a banner hanging between two trees. It reads: LOVE IS LOVE. I roll my eyes at it, wishing it were so easy.

In the cold, I find the back-to-front name carved into the bark of a tree. Loving them was an idea planted in my mind. I liked the conundrum and our study sessions, but relief washed over me when love did not boil.

There are two grey squirrels on a bird table. They have human faces and are kissing each other. I find kissing a strange act.

'Would you like to kiss someone someday?' asks one of the squirrels.

'At twenty-seven, you'd have thought it would have happened by now,' states the other.

I take a moment to reflect on the question posed by the human-faced squirrels.

'Maybe I would kiss someone, but I'm not missing out,' I reply, 'Maybe if kissing wasn't so exclusive. People must enjoy it, but it comes with so much emotional baggage.'

'Maybe if kissing was more casual?' prods a squirrel.

'Perhaps.'

The warmth of friendship is wonderful enough. Friendship comes with beautiful and intense feelings. Me and my best friend in primary school used to nuzzle our noses together. Or 'elephant kisses', as my mum would call it. I remember her teaching me how. It's where we would press the tips of our noses together and rub them from one side to the other. My friend and I often added to this show of affection with hugs and giggles. I've since wondered if me and my friend had kissed, and this lesson of elephants was some form of halfway deterrent. But I can't remember.

Further through the forest, I enter a snowy clearing to an audience in deck chairs. I stand in front of them and speak:

'I didn't want them to love me, 'cause I couldn't reciprocate. But, as our friendship bloomed, so did a desired intimacy. Heavy feelings weighed me down. An unromantic, platonic sexual desire. This took me so long to learn. School fails queer children.' I sigh, looking out at the bored faces of the crowd, then continue. 'My last date was a year ago. He was cute, he was cool, and quick to emphasise a lack of "spark".'

'You're Aromantic Demisexual, friend,' someone from the audience shouts out.

'Shut up, gay boy!'

The audience fight among themselves, and I leave.

A magician once convinced a girl that I loved her. I was chased for weeks with heart-shaped rocks. Magicians are awful.

My thoughts are awash with my love of research and writing. The arts own my loveless body.

'What about friends?' I ask myself.

'That's a given,' I scold. 'Friendships come above all else.'

I walk boldly forward, carrying my successes and failures as they are. I am still in search of a combination of letters which fit together. A concoction of phonetics which feel good as they press up against my throat. I feel the words wander around my mouth, and one day I'll cast these spellings with magical meaning.

A Life Lived in Secret
Kate Foot

CW: mild internalised homophobia, mentions of death and grief

Ruth had lived for almost a century.

A lifetime of hiding, of never knowing who was safe and where was safe, who would bring judgement and where would bring violence. A lifetime of never being her true, authentic self. A lifetime of lies, packed into boxes and suitcases and carried along with her from one home to the next to the next, unable ever to be unpacked and proudly displayed beside her treasured family photographs and cherished chosen ornaments.

She carried those lies everywhere.

But they were heavy and she was tired and her time was running out.

She needed to put them down.

*

The world had moved on. She was a fossil, now, old and decrepit and still carrying her secrets deep within her ruins.

She grew up in a village in the valleys of South Wales, in a small house with no electricity, heated only by an old coal fire. It had been quiet. Insular. Full of expectations.

Not/Coming Out

You went to the village school. You helped on the farm or in the shop on a Saturday. Church on Sunday. You took your annual holiday at the beach, an hour's ride away on the 42 bus. You met a nice boy, perhaps from a neighbouring village, and you married him and bore his children and you kept house like a good wife should, and then you died and everyone said lovely things at your funeral.

Expectations that made little Ruthie want to scream.

Expectations that were still there, even though the world had changed, now abuzz with electricity and traffic noise and information and people dashing everywhere.

Ruth hadn't been able to keep up with it all, even before she had to come into this godforsaken nursing home with its overly cheerful staff. Oh, she was grateful enough for the care, she supposed, but it was a loss of privacy and space and as her independence was eroded, she felt her sense of self slipping away along with it.

She clung to the one thing that no one could take away from her.

Her secret.

The one she had carried for a lifetime, packed into its own special box. The heaviest one of all.

But was it really a secret when a small, select few had known?

A handful of girls, those she had stolen kisses with outside dark village halls when the dance was over and the couples had left. They had laughed and called her silly, or said it was good practice for when one of the boys finally wanted to kiss them, and then they'd talked with a dreamy voice about finding the beau of their dreams and what he might look like; or about the object of their affections, someone they knew and were hoping to catch the eye of.

Ruth couldn't understand that. The only object of her affection at that time was one Elizabeth Masters – and as she was already engaged to be married, any pursuit of romance with her was pointless.

Pointless and wrong.

That was a lesson Ruth had learned young. She was wrong. She would never be accepted the way she was. She had to fit in, carve off pieces of herself and fulfil the expectations that were forced upon her.

And so she did.

She joined the war effort; she moved away from her home to a nearby town, and used the tailoring skills learned from her father to make uniforms for the soldiers. There she met David, at a dance that had been cut short by an air raid siren shrieking its warning. He had helped her to put out the lights and offered to walk her home.

Ruth had gracefully accepted. One couldn't be too careful out here, with no streetlights, and he seemed like a decent sort of chap. A funny one, too, she'd discovered by the time they reached her boarding house a few streets away. So when he politely asked her for a date, she had accepted that, too, in keeping with the expectations of a civilised society.

But she never dreamed of him the way the other girls dreamed of their beaus.

She didn't think of him like that at all.

When he wanted to kiss her, she agreed, and did her best to kiss him back. When he wanted more, she batted him away and sternly told him 'not before marriage'. When he proposed marriage, she said yes.

It would be the perfect cover.

No one would suspect her secret if she had a husband.

She supposed she loved him, in her own way. She loved him enough to give him what he wanted on their wedding night, and after; and he had given her a beautiful baby boy who they called Matthew.

Ruth loved him with her whole heart. This sweet little innocent baby who had done no wrong and would maybe grow up to be like her and she wouldn't be alone anymore.

It didn't turn out like that, though.

After the war was over, David was keen to return to his family in London and Ruth obliged him. The bright lights of the big city brought anonymity and independence and hope.

Maybe there were others like her here.

With so many people around, she surely couldn't be the only one.

But she was a married woman with a babe in arms, and opportunities to meet new people were limited.

At least the baby gave her an excuse. Between night time feedings and nappy changes, the opportunities for David to get his hands on her were limited and on the occasions he did try, she bashed him away and told him she wasn't in the mood.

He was a patient man and took it well, but his patience only stretched so far. Ruth accepted his first affair. And his second. She was relieved he wasn't pestering her for things she didn't want to give him. But by the third, she seized her opportunity.

Even a judgemental society would accept a divorce after three affairs.

Oh, there was still a certain amount of judgement. Divorced women were shunned, but there was less judgement over a divorce than over the other thing. Her secret. If that came out, her life would be ruined.

Better to be a jilted wife who stood up to the injustices of her husband's affairs than a lesbian, at least in the eyes of those around her.

So then it was just her and Matthew. He was seven years old by then. He didn't really understand very much, but he accepted things and he helped her around the house and she taught him to cook and do housework because Ruth didn't see why those things had to be women's work. She was damned if she was going to raise a son who couldn't do anything for himself.

Not/Coming Out

As he grew up, though, he started to see the cracks in her carefully plastered facade. She could never be her true self, not even around him, and he sensed that barrier between them. What sort of mother was she? She should be able to love her child, but how could she love him when she had a mask glued firmly in place, one that he would never be able to see her without?

He began to distance himself, as though he was responding to the emotional distance by creating physical distance between them. He moved out, moved in with his father and his father's fancy woman, but he soon came back because he wasn't wanted there.

Ruth's heart ached for him, but she could never tell him who she really was.

And things were never the same.

She hadn't done a good enough job of hiding it and it had pushed Matthew away.

She let him go. It was for his own good. Let him go and be free and meet someone and be happy.

He did, and he was, but their relationship never recovered.

The secret was too big. Too heavy. No relationship could survive that.

Ruth would never know unconditional love and acceptance. Not while she was still lugging around that big old secret in that big old box.

She was destined to be alone.

But at least she was free.

Not/Coming Out

Insofar as she ever was.

*

She found people. A code had developed, a way of figuring out who was safe and who wasn't; who she could be herself with and who she couldn't.

A simple question.

Are you family?

A simple question but a safe one. One that gave nothing away and was easily explained.

'Are you family?' she would ask, and if the response was a puzzled look and an 'I don't think so', she would brush it off with an apology and an explanation that the person looked just like a cousin she hadn't seen for years. No one ever raised an eyebrow at that.

'Are you family?' she would ask, and if the response was a warm smile and a 'Yes, I am', she would breathe a sigh of relief and know she was safe with them.

She could be herself. Her true self. No one asked how or why she was family, it was enough to ask that question and receive that answer and they would know she was one of them. Acceptance without having to reveal her secret.

She kept her secret safe, even with those she called family. She kept it safe inside that big heavy box because no one needed to know the details.

Until she met Virginia.

*

Beautiful, brilliant Virginia.

Not/Coming Out

'Are you family?'

A warm smile. 'Yes, I am.'

A simple, safe question that sparked a friendship and then a date and then more. More than little Ruthie could have ever dreamed of, and more than adult Ruth could have ever hoped for.

The brightest, purest love that she had ever known.

Both retired by then and with time on their hands, they had nothing to do except love each other in the way they had both been missing for so long.

Virginia's story mirrored her own. A husband, long since gone. Children, alienated by their strange, closed off mother.

A life lived alone.

A secret carried for a lifetime.

But now they had each other. They did everything together. Coffee mornings and keep-fit classes for the old people and day trips and holidays in hotel rooms with twin beds that they pushed together as one.

With Virginia, Ruth found the acceptance she had craved for so many years. She found peace and a love that she didn't know could even exist, one that burned bright with safety and warmth, that felt like curling up by the fire on a stormy night, sheltered from the wind and rain outside.

And she found herself.

She learned to see herself through Virginia's eyes, learned to accept the love that Virginia gave her, learned to accept who she was and that she wasn't bad or wrong or anything else that the world had made her believe she was.

They hid themselves from that world. The one that was so cruel and harsh and full of judgement.

'We're just good friends,' they would say.

'She's my best friend.'

It wasn't even a lie. They were the best of friends, the way all good relationships should be.

Ruth was sure people guessed. Her parents were long gone, but her siblings must have known. Matthew too, probably. Her friends, those she didn't call family – she thought some of them might have figured it out.

But she didn't tell them. She couldn't say it out loud. If she did, maybe she would lose it, maybe she and Virginia would crumble under the weight of their judgement and the bright light of their love would be snuffed out like a church candle. If they guessed on their own, if they drew their own conclusions or made their own assumptions, well, that was none of her business.

So she kept quiet and kept referring to Virginia as her best friend, and she kept dreaming of a world without judgement where they would be free to live as openly as a married couple.

Until fifteen years later when it was all ripped away.

*

Virginia. Beautiful, lovely, wonderful Virginia.

The first in a long line of losses.

Oh, she had lost people before that. Her parents, of course. A handful of friends. Some of the few men she had called family, taken by the sickness that had plagued them.

But no one close.

No one like Virginia.

That loss was almost unbearable. She'd heard people describe it as like losing a limb or having their heart or stomach torn out, but not for Ruth.

For Ruth, it was more quiet. A hollowness. An utter certainty that she would never be the same again. That she was empty and lost, without direction or gravity, just floating. Existing.

Her life ended that day, too.

She would never recover from the loss of her beloved Virginia.

*

Ruth had lived too long. She knew that. Almost a century. It wasn't fair to have to live for that long. Not after all her loved ones had gone.

Virginia, twenty years before, the pain still as sharp as that awful day. Her siblings, scattered along the way. Her Matthew, just a year before, taken by a short illness while he was still young, at least compared to her. It wasn't right for a mother to lose a child like that.

So much loss.

So much grief.

So much emptiness.

Not/Coming Out

She was ready for it to end now.

It wouldn't be long. Her time was close. She could feel it. Her body was slowly giving up, her mind along with it. It wouldn't be long now.

Her secret still weighed heavily, still packed inside its box that she carried everywhere with her. She didn't want to die with it. She wanted to put it down and leave it behind so she could move on in peace.

There was only one person left to tell. All of her friends were gone. Dead, or gone, the day she moved into this godforsaken nursing home. Even her nieces and nephews had started to die off – and anyway, she wasn't close to them. So there was only one person.

Her granddaughter.

Matthew's daughter, Nicole. Now somewhere in her forties – Ruth couldn't remember exactly. A nice girl. Caring. Practical. Not prone to flights of fancy or emotions. She would take it well, Ruth was sure.

But still.

Still.

Could she face the heartbreak of being rejected by the only family she had left? Of being cast out purely for the crime of loving who she had loved? Could she trust that the new generation was more tolerant, that she would find a smile and acceptance instead of harsh words like bad and wrong or worse?

She spent days agonising over it. She turned it over and over in her mind, carefully examining it from all angles so she could prepare herself for whatever response Nicole gave her. She decided she could do it. She decided she couldn't do it. She decided she could do it again.

Each day would bring a new decision, a surety that no she couldn't or yes she could and by the next day, she'd changed her mind again, only to change it back once more.

Eventually, she had a nurse help her to phone Nicole.

'Oh, hello dear. I was wondering if you could come up this weekend, there's something I need to talk to you about.'

'Of course, Nan,' Nicole said, her voice warm even through the tinny phone line. 'I'll be up on Sunday, how about I bring a picnic lunch?'

'That sounds lovely, dear. I'll see you then.'

The nurse took the phone away and Ruth was left with her thoughts.

She could always change her mind, tell Nicole about something else, some barely remembered story from the past that didn't matter. But she wouldn't.

She would, in modern day parlance, come out to her granddaughter.

It would be safe now, she thought. Now that the world had moved on. Some of the nurses wore rainbow pins, a little symbol of the community that she called family. She thought there was more acceptance these days.

She hoped so, anyway.

Not/Coming Out

She didn't think she could bear to be rejected when she had such little time remaining on this earth.

*

'What did you want to talk about, Nan?' Nicole asked as they were munching on some fancy sandwiches that she'd picked up from Marks and Spencer.

Ruth liked Marks and Spencer. It was a bit pricey but there was no waste with it. She hated waste, especially wasted food, but Marks and Spencer food was always good.

'Hmm?' she said, looking up from her sandwich. 'Well, it's nothing really, dear. It's just a little thing.'

'Okay, so tell me the little thing and then we'll have those cakes.'

Fancy little butterfly cupcakes with raspberry jam and icing. Ruth was looking forward to those. Far nicer than the Victoria sponge that the nursing home kitchen usually served up. Not that she was complaining – any cake was good cake, but these ones looked extra special and tasty.

'Well, dear, it really is nothing, I just wanted to tell you that I'm a lesbian.'

A warm smile grew on Nicole's face. 'Thank you for trusting me with that. I bet you've been carrying that for a while.'

Ruth nodded. 'It was getting rather heavy. I thought you should know. You don't mind?'

'Of course not. That makes us family.'

That word. That beautiful word that meant so much. Not just family, but family.

Ruth's eyes were stinging with the weight of unshed tears that threatened to break free and then Nicole's hand was warm on her arm, calm and comforting, and Ruth allowed the tears to cascade down her cheeks. There was no point holding them in anymore.

She sobbed, letting go of so many years of secrets and lies and hiding. She put down the boxes, put them to one side to unpack later, and took a good look around. There was so much space inside her with all of those boxes gone, space that she would soon learn to fill so that she wouldn't feel so hollow anymore. Now she could be filled with love instead of secrets, and hope instead of lies.

Nicole held her hand while she cried, and gave her a tissue to dry her eyes afterwards. Ruth tapped a tiny rainbow flag pin that Nicole wore on her jacket. She'd never noticed it before.

'Can you get me one of those?'

'I can do better than that.' Nicole unclipped it and held it out to Ruth. 'Do you want to wear it or just keep it with you?'

'I want to wear it.'

Nicole smiled and pinned it onto Ruth's blouse. Ruth straightened her collar, practically beaming with pride.

In the twilight of her life, she had found acceptance. She could unpack all of those boxes, take out every part of herself and display them alongside the family photos and ornaments. There was no judgement anymore.

No more hiding.

No more lies.

No more secrets.

She was loved and accepted.

Just as she was.

Loving Emily
Florence-Susanne Reppert

I told her once I hated how she'd equate our middle school basement kisses to us being 'so weird'.

'It's not like we're gay,' she'd say,
speaking against my mouth between gasping breaths,
mid-pubescent, starving bodies entwined on her parents couch as if we belonged there.
Hidden amongst the embroidered roses.
I'd cringe as her words heaved across my tongue, pushing her shame down my throat,
Her self hatred burning, threatening to spread like a homo-necrotic disease.

Forcing a smile, I'd chuckle.
'Yeah. You're right.'

It's not like I'm gay.
It's not like I find my eyes drawn to the curve of your body and wish I could kiss every mile of skin between us.
It's not like my heart seizes with every tinkling cackle of your laughter.

Not/Coming Out

Every twirl of hair around those perfectly delicate fingers.

It's not like I'm in love with every.

Single.

Thing.

You.

Do.

But I don't say any of that.

I just smile, pulling her closer.

Laughing off the gay and holding on to every curiosity she satiates with my coward's heart.

We're not coming out today.

Or even tomorrow.

I will keep your secret, tucking it away in the back of the closet.

Behind the winter clothes that don't fit and I was too self conscious to wear.

Under the board games we lost all the pieces to and never bothered to find.

Hidden beneath every single aspect of my life I kept from everyone.

Not/Coming Out

Loving you, Emily, is worth hiding this part of me,
of us,
for a little while longer.

Quite the Actor
Felix Graves

She tells me I cannot act
flat expressions don't
move masses to tears
but I try
and I try
and I cannot agree
disguising internalized torture
twisting it into beatitude
is my forté

Mother tells me I cannot sing
my throat doesn't create
dulcet tones of harmony and grace
but I try
and I try
and I cannot agree
deluges of transient notes
liberate me, libate me

something stifled housewives
cannot grasp

Not/Coming Out

She tells me I cannot draw
shaking hands bring forth
only faults and flaws
but I try
and I try
and I cannot agree
the influx of creativity illuminates
a darkness hidden within

a Secret

She tells me I cannot write
my words tossed on paper
jumbled
into an incongruous incorrigible mess
but I try
and I try
and I cannot agree
pen sculpts papier-mâché worlds
full of identities she couldn't
possibly comprehend

She tells me I am girl
Woman
holy vessel, majestic womb, pristine...
tamed and trusted to blossom
but I try
and I try

Not/Coming Out

and I cannot agree
bows and bustles trussed
perfectly presentable for Him?

will I find a word for
what – who I am?

She tells me I am beautiful
a tiny model of her
one quintessential little
wife in the making
but I try
and I try
and I cannot agree
I am other, dressed up in
picturesque pink and pearly white
wrongly packaged at birth

Why do you say I can't act
Mother?
when my performance
in femininity has
fooled
even
you

Cruising
Felix Graves

Mists cradle you, perpetuating a swaddling darkness:
dim and dewy. And the sounds – *OOOOOO* –
echoing, answering, piercing stillness and vapor.
Letting you know

I'm out here
You're not invisible
to me

Strangers passing safely in the night beneath a blanket
of fog so beautiful you forget it's hiding monsters, held
at bay by our calls

A lighthouse glows in the distance, illuminating a way
of safety. And you long to step into the iridescence,
emerge, be seen

even for a second

But shadows envelope you, a lifelong friend – *It's not*
your time – cocooned, safe for a little while longer

96

Not/Coming Out

A foghorn sounds close by and before you manifests
the most glorious ship, resplendent in its pride, and
you long for it to see you, to catch a glimpse… Instead,
you sound your horn and it responds in kind

Even though you are not seen, what comfort to hear
your presence is accepted, known. You are not lost but
found. Despite being hidden in the shadows

You exist

Author Biographies
in anthology order

Nil Digante
He/They

Nil Digante is a queer, Desi-American writer who likes to write about the places where the different parts of their identity intersects. When not writing, he likes to sing, play the ukulele, and send long info-dumps to his friends and partners. You can find them on Twitter @nil_digante or Insta @nil_digante0.

Colin Brooks
He/Him

Colin Brooks is a queer author from Florida, now living in Maryland, and graduate from the University of Central Florida, where he earned his two Bachelors of Arts degrees in Creative Writing and Theatre Studies. In 2021, he published his debut novel, Paint, a contemporary fiction coming-of-age story about

Not/Coming Out

discovering one's queerness and the world of drag. You can find him on all social media @colinbrooksbooks.

Katherine Shaw
She/Her

Katherine Shaw is a multi-genre writer, bi and grey ace disaster, and self-confessed nerd, hailing from Yorkshire in the UK. She spends most of her time dreaming up new characters or playing D&D, and you can find more about her and her latest work at her website (www.katherineshawwrites.com).

Priscilla Kint
She/Her

Priscilla Kint (she/her) is a Dutch author of short stories and Young Adult fiction. She completed the MA Creative Writing at Bath Spa University in 2018 and has had work published by Luna Station Quarterly, Sley House, Bag of Bones Press, and Inkling of Thunder. Her stories usually include LGBTQIA+ representation (most notably aro/ace characters), headstrong teenagers, and a hint of magic. She also occasionally dabbles in spoken word poetry. In

Not/Coming Out

her spare time, she likes to cuddle with her dog Balou and pretend she can play the piano. You can find her on Twitter: @priscillareads.

Breanna Guinta
She/Her

Breanna K. Guinta is a college student studying English. She has poems published in Monmouth Review Issue 66 and Treasured 2017 Poetry Collection by America Library of Poetry. When she isn't writing, she could be found spending time with her fur-babies, watching anime or with her head in a good book.

Airic Fenn
They/Them

Airic Fenn is a child of the Rocky Mountains and spends more of their time in their own vivid imaginings than perhaps is proper (but who really cares about proper?). When they aren't writing, you can find them making art or dabbling in one of their many hobbies, from leathercraft and bookbinding to exploring the outdoors and attending renfaires.

Not/Coming Out

Samantha Maich
She/Her

Samantha Maich is the author of What is Zaida Dreaming, The ABCs of Halloween, and Where Will Leon Explore. A fierce advocate for LGBTQIA+ causes, she participates in local advocacy groups and events to help create a safe space for all to be their authentic selves. Samantha can be found at home crafting next to her two adorable yet feral cats, or on her website www.samanthamaich.com.

Robyn Hill
She/Her

Robyn Hill is a lesbian poet and screenwriter from the UK. Her writing features themes such as nostalgia, sexuality, the world ending, cats, all that good stuff. Through her work, she aims to document a range of queer stories whilst increasing the representation of LGBTQ+ writers across all forms. You can find her on Instagram, Twitter, and YouTube @robyynnhill.

Not/Coming Out

Emily Byars
She/Her

Emily Byars is currently a graduate student residing in Mobile, Alabama, USA completing her master's degree in creative writing. She was recently named the winner of the Stokes Award for Creative Nonfiction and has served on the editing staff of Oracle Fine Arts Review since 2021. This is her first publication.

Sarah Fletchins
She/They

Sarah Fletchins is a demi-pansexual genderfluid British-Australian human (who may or may not be a dragon on the inside) living in the UK, where she is constantly in awe of proper changes of season, squirrels and 'part time trees.' She lives in Sheffield with her husband and two adopted rabbit fur children. There she can usually be found drinking too much tea, making artwork, reading stories aloud to grown-ups, singing rock songs or lost in a forest. Her work includes writing of short fiction for her 'Storytime for Grown-Ups' project, poetry, YA queer supernatural romance, and various illustration, photography and general creativity. She is passionate about nature, tea, the queer community, creativity, and love.

Sky DuVall
They/He

Sky DuVall is an introvert who spends most of their time writing and consuming books and media to find new ways to tell stories and be inspired. They are currently working on their first book. When not getting bullied by their two cats, Sky likes to walk in nature and contemplate what role stories have in a world that constantly changes.

A. Lynn Rosefinch
He/Him

Artie is a gender-fluid writer of both poetry and prose. His work tends to feature themes of childhood, queerness, and finding belonging, usually with ghosts. When he's not writing, Artie is usually playing Ace Attorney, hanging out with his partner, coaching slam poetry, or working as a mascot performer.

Not/Coming Out

Hannah Rose
She/Her

Hannah Rose has been writing and creating art ever since she could hold a pen, but she has yet to land upon a genre to stick to. If you can't find her scribbling furiously in a beautiful notebook, you'll find her drawing, being a mama or daydreaming about the Scottish wilderness that holds her heart.

Brandon Shane
He/Him

Brandon Shane is a Japanese-American alum of California State University, Long Beach, where he majored in English. He's pursuing an MFA while working as a writing instructor and substitute teacher. You can see his work in the Berlin Literary Review, Acropolis Journal, Grim & Gilded, Livina Press, Messy Misfits, Remington Review, Mister Magazine, Discretionary Love, among many others. Find him on Twitter @Ruishanewrites

Not/Coming Out

Daniel Skentelbery
He/Him

Daniel Skentelbery (he/him) is a writer, artist, and researcher. He recently passed his PhD in Media, Communications and Culture from Keele University. At the age of 27, whilst submitting his PhD, Daniel came out as AroAce (Aromantic Asexual). Coming out to himself was a long road and the hardest thing he has ever done, but he is grateful to be here now. His first poetry collection Miss Peacock and the Actress was published in 2022. Daniel enjoys painting rabbits, the music of dodie, and his favourite Pokémon are Plusle and Minun.

Kate Foot
She/Her

Kate lives in the Forest of Dean with her husband, three dogs and a cat. She is queer, autistic, disabled, and spends an inordinate amount of time arguing with chronic illness about what she's allowed to do today.

Not/Coming Out

Florence-Susanne Reppert
They/Them

Florence-Susanne is a 26 year old non-binary/Pansexual Poet, Photographer, parent, and EIC of Poetry as Promised Magazine. They host Nowhere as Promised open mic and you can find them online under Schizo_trash_poet.

Felix Graves
He/Him

Felix Graves is a queer, trans, and disabled AAPI author. He whiles away his days by dreaming up stories of tragic faeries, bloodthirsty pirates, and messy queers. His horror stories have been included in various anthologies published by Lost Boys Press, Autumn Nights, and Dark Dispatch, and his poetry has been published in several online zines. He lives in the beautiful PNW with his husband, two kids, and his trusty and cuddly pitbull.

Artist Biographies

Yasemin Anders
She/They

Writer of kissing books; illustrator and artist.

EM Harding
They/Them

Em is a queer disabled artist and writer who hails from Wales! When not scribbling on the backs of discarded receipts, Em can be found engaging in a 9-5 of computer husbandry and coffee, eating one too many bourbon biscuits and/or walking a tiny magician named Merlin. You can find their books, Labours of Stone (2021) and Moon-Sitting (2019), on Amazon now!

Not/Coming Out

Dewi Hargreaves
He/Him

Dewi is an illustrator from the cold, soggy middle of the UK. He's worked on over 200 maps for the front matter of books, and he's a big fan of The Elder Scrolls and cheese.

Kickstarter Acknowledgements

Sarah Bell
Liam Studders
Mina Molloy (A.M. Molloy)
Angelique Madere
Airic Fenn
El Horgan
Rae OHW
Lucia Judinova
Andrew McEwen
Lindsey Petrucci
Stephen Howard

Thank you to all our Kickstarter supporters!

Full Credits

Authors

Nil Digante
Colin Brooks
Katherine Shaw
Priscilla Kint
Breanna Guinta
Airic Fenn
Samantha Maich
Robyn Hill
Emily Byars
Sarah Fletchins
Sky DuVall
A. Lynn Rosefinch
Hannah Rose
Brandon Shane
Daniel Skentelbery
Kate Foot
Florence-Susanne Reppert
Felix Graves

Not/Coming Out

Editors

Amanda Shortman
Kenzie Millar
Dewi Hargreaves
Lou Willingham

Artists

Yasemin Anders
EM Harding
Dewi Hargreaves
Bee Smith

Supporters

Macfarlane Lantern Publishing
Kickstarter
Mj
Early readers
Reviewers

Not/Coming Out

Resources
Please note that this is not an exhaustive list.

General LGBTQIA+ charities, organisations, and websites

All Out
https://allout.org/en
All Out is an international movement fighting for LGBTQ+ rights across the globe.

GLAAD
https://glaad.org/
GLAAD is a non-profit organization focused on LGBTQ advocacy and cultural change.

FFLAG
https://www.fflag.org.uk/
FFLAG is a charity that is dedicated to supporting families and their LGBT+ members.

ILGA
https://ilga.org/
ILGA - The International Lesbian, Gay, Bisexual, Trans, and Intersex Association, is a worldwide federation which has been championing LGBT+ rights globally since 1978.

Kaleidoscope Trust
https://kaleidoscopetrust.com/

Not/Coming Out

Kaleidoscope Trust is a UK-based international charity working towards a future where LGBTI+ people everywhere can live free, safe, and equal lives.

LGBT Foundation
https://lgbt.foundation/
LGBT Foundation is a national charity that supports the health and wellbeing of the LGBTQ+ Community.

LGBT Hero
https://www.lgbthero.org.uk/
LGBT Hero is a national health and wellbeing charity, supporting over 100,000 people a month.

Stonewall
https://www.stonewall.org.uk/
Stonewall is an organisation that fights for the rights of LGBTQ+ people.

Switchboard
https://switchboard.lgbt/
Switchboard is a national LGBTQIA+ support line for anyone at any stage of their journey.

Specific LGBTQIA+ Identities

Asexual Outreach
https://asexualoutreach.org/
Asexual Outreach is a non-profit that works to build awareness of ace identities and build communities.

Not/Coming Out

The Asexual Visibility and Education Network (AVEN)
https://www.asexuality.org/
AVEN hosts an online asexuality community forum as well as providing lots of resources on asexuality.

Bi Pride UK
https://biprideuk.org/
Bi Pride UK's mission is to create a space where people who experience attraction beyond gender can be freely visible and celebrate themselves.

Mermaids
https://mermaidsuk.org.uk/
Mermaids is a charity that supports trans, non-binary, and gender diverse children, young people, and their families.

Not A Phase
https://notaphase.org/
Not A Phase is a trans led grassroots movement whose aim is to uplift and improve the lives of trans adults.

Sparkle
https://www.sparkle.org.uk/
Sparkle is a national transgender charity that hosts Sparkle Weekend in Manchester and undertakes projects throughout the year to further its aims of promoting a positive representation of the trans, non-binary/genderfluid, and intersex community.

Not/Coming Out

LGBTQIA+ Youth

akt
https://www.akt.org.uk/
akt is a charity that helps provide safe routes to housing and support for LGBTQ+ youth.
All profits from the sale of this anthology are being donated to akt.

Just Like Us
https://www.justlikeus.org/
Just Like Us is an LGBT+ charity that aims to empower young people to be role models by connecting university students to schools where they can share their LGBT+ stories.

LGBTQIA+ Mental Health

Galop
https://galop.org.uk/
Galop is a national helpline for LGBT+ victims and survivors of abuse and violence.

Mind Out
https://mindout.org.uk/
Mind Out is a mental health service run by and for members of the LGBTQIA+ Community.

The Trevor Project
https://www.thetrevorproject.org/

Not/Coming Out

The Trevor Project is a suicide prevention and crisis intervention non-profit, offering LGBTQ+ youth access to support 24/7, all year round.

LGBTQIA+, Faith & Religion

Galva-108
https://www.galva108.org/
Galva-108 provides information and support for LGBTI Vaishnavas and Hindus.

Hidayah UK
https://hidayahlgbt.com/
Hidayah UK provides support for LGBTQ+ Muslims and promotes education about the community.

Inclusive Mosque
https://inclusivemosque.org/
The Inclusive Mosque Initiative is an intersectional feminist mosque dedicated to creating inclusive, safe places for marginalised Muslims and their families.

Keshet UK
https://www.keshetuk.org/
Keshet UK has a vision of a world where nobody is forced to choose between their LGBT+ and Jewish identity.

Naz and Matt Foundation
https://www.nazandmattfoundation.org/

Not/Coming Out

Naz and Matt Foundation works to remove the barriers that prevent religious and culturally conservative parents from accepting their LGBTQI+ children.

OneBodyOneFaith
https://www.onebodyonefaith.org.uk/
OneBodyOneFaith is a grassroots charity that enables LGBT+ Christians to advocate for change within the church.

Quest
https://questlgbti.uk/
Quest exists to provide pastoral support to LGBT+ Catholics.

Sarbat
https://www.sarbat.net/
Sarbat is a volunteer-led group addressing LGBT+ issues from a Sikh perspective.

Twilight People
https://www.twilightpeople.com/
Twilight People is a landmark project that discovers and celebrates the hidden history of transgender and gender-variant people of faith in the UK. It brings together the stories of over 40 members of the various Abrahamic faith communities - Jewish, Christian, and Muslim.

LGBTQIA+ Black and People of Colour

Center for Black Equality

Not/Coming Out

https://centerforblackequity.org/
Center for Black Equality is a charity that focuses on improving the lives of Black LGBTQ+ people globally.

Colours Youth Network
https://www.coloursyouthnetwork.com/
Colours Youth Network uplifts, supports, and empowers young people of colour between the ages of 16 and 25 who are also LGBTQI to explore and celebrate who they are.

House of Rainbow
https://www.houseofrainbow.org
House of Rainbow works to create a place of safety for black LGBTQI+ people of faith.

Regional (UK) LGBTQIA+ charities and groups

London Gaymers
https://londongaymers.co.uk/
London Gaymers is a safe space for the LGBT+ gaming community in London and across the UK. They hold various social events in London and have a Discord server and Facebook group.

Metro
https://metrocharity.org.uk/
Metro is an equality, diversity, and inclusive services charity working in London, Essex, Kent, Medway, Surrey, and West Sussex.

Not/Coming Out

Mosaic Trust
https://www.mosaictrust.org.uk/
Mosaic Trust is a charity that aims to support, educate, and inspire London's LGBT+ Youth.

The Outside Project
https://lgbtiqoutside.org/
The Outside Project is an LGBTQI+ Community Shelter, Centre, and Domestic Abuse Refuge in London.

The Proud Trust
https://www.theproudtrust.org/
The Proud Trust is an LGBT+ youth charity working within Greater Manchester.

Think2Speak
https://www.think2speak.com/
Think2Speak works with LGBTQ+ children, young people, and families within Lincolnshire.

Awareness Days
Please note that this is not an exhaustive list.

February

All month - LGBT+ History Month (UK)
Begins Sunday after Valentine's Day - Aromantic
Spectrum Awareness Week

March

All month - Bisexual Health Awareness Month
1st - Zero Discrimination Day
First Saturday - Mardi Gras Parade (Australia)
31st - International Transgender Day of Visibility

April

6th - International Asexuality Day
12th - Day of Silence (US)
Week incl. 26th - Lesbian Visibility Week
26th - Lesbian Visibility Day

Not/Coming Out

May

All month - Queer History Month (Berlin)
17th - International Day Against Homophobia,
Transphobia, and Biphobia
19th - Agender Pride Day
24th - Pansexual Visibility Day

June

All month - Pride Month
5th - HIV Long Term Survivor's Awareness Day
28th - Stonewall Riots Anniversary

July

6th - Omnisexual Visibility Day
14th - International Non-Binary Awareness Day
Week incl. 14th - Non-Binary Awareness Week
16th - International Drag Day

August

Second Sunday - Gay Uncles (Guncles) Day

September

Week incl. 23rd - Bisexual Awareness Week
23rd - Bi Visibility Day

Not/Coming Out

October

All month - LGBT History Month (Australia, USA and Canada)
8th - International Lesbian Day (Australia and New Zealand)
11th - National Coming Out Day
Third Wednesday - International Pronoun Day
Third Thursday - Spirit Day
Last full week of the month - Asexual Awareness Week (Ace Week)
26th - Intersex Awareness Day

November

All month - Transgender Awareness Month
First Sunday - Transgender Parent Day
8th - Intersex Day of Remembrance
13-19th Transgender Awareness Week
20th - Transgender Day of Remembrance (TDOR)

December

1st - World AIDS Day
8th - Pansexual Pride Day
10th - Human Rights Day

AKT

Akt helps LGBTQ+ young people find safety and security. They do this by providing pathways into safe housing and access to social support and also assist with routes into training and employment.

In a little over 30 years, they've created a national network of safe places and digital support services. Their relationships with other incredible charities allow us to support thousands of young people every year.

Supporters keep their vital services running.

100% of royalties from the sale of Not/Coming Out are being donated directly to akt.

Buying this book helps akt achieve their mission to provide routes to safer housing and support for LGBTQ+ young people.

Thank you!

—

Printed in Great Britain
by Amazon